Companion in Faith

The Beatitudes

Kathleen M. Basi

Our Sunday Visitor
Huntington, Indiana

Our Sunday Visitor Publishing Division
Our Sunday Visitor, Inc. .
200 Noll Plaza
Huntington, IN 46750
www.osv.com
1-800-348-2440

ISBN: 978-1-68192-465-6 (Inventory No. T2348)
LCCN: 2019934652

Cover design: Tyler Ottinger
Cover art: Shutterstock.com
Interior design: Lindsey Riesen

PRINTED IN THE UNITED STATES OF AMERICA

INTRODUCTION

Jesus' Beatitudes (the word means "blessedness" or "supreme happiness") encapsulate the Gospel in compact form: they describe the heart of God. The Beatitudes issue a deep challenge to each of us and provide us with directions for finding blessedness in discipleship.

This booklet will guide you through using the Beatitudes in examining your life and actions. You can use it as an examination of conscience, as a guide for reflection, or simply as a way to enter more deeply into the life of blessedness the Lord wants to give us as his children. This booklet will invite you to meditate deeply on Jesus' teachings about Christian living. You might spend a day or two reflecting on how each Beatitude speaks into your life. A small journal would be perfect for gathering your responses.

Matthew and Luke present slightly different versions of some of the Beatitudes, so in some cases we will dig into the two versions separately.

Meditating on each Beatitude, you will first *focus inward*, examining your heart for attitudes and thoughts that do not align with the heart of Christ. Next, you will *focus outward*, because our words and actions give form to what lies within our hearts. In each section, ask yourself: How does this Beatitude play out in today's world? How are you called to view, interact with, or respond to others in light of this Beatitude? Finally, you'll synthesize your reflections and bring them to the Lord in *prayer*, asking him to help you identify what the *next step* might be.

Don't rush this process. Take time to live with the reflections, ponder the questions, and sit with God in prayer. The questions are tough, but that's because living the Faith intentionally in the real world is tough. May this booklet lead you toward the blessedness — the closeness to the heart of God — that Christ laid out for us.

·· 1 ··

*"Blessed are the poor in spirit, for theirs is
the kingdom of heaven." — Matthew 5:3*

FOCUS INWARD: **Recognizing My Attachment
to the Things of the World**

Right from the beginning of the Sermon on the
Mount, Jesus makes it clear that discipleship is
anything but business as usual. In this first Beatitude as recorded in Matthew, he praises those
who are not just poor, but poor *in spirit*. This
suggests something deeper than material poverty. It suggests humility; it suggests detachment
and self-emptying. It suggests seeking spiritual
rather than material riches and trusting in God
and his providence.

To cultivate a heart that is not bound to
the things of the world is a challenge, to say the

least. Our economy depends upon consumption, so the line between needs and wants can become blurry. Being generous in our giving to the Church and to the needy can be frightening. If material luxuries aren't a pitfall, plenty of other worldly interests can trip us up. There's pride — a feeling that I am owed a certain level of respect or deference, a sense of self-importance and self-sufficiency. Maybe I have the tendency to become angry when I am crossed because I feel too important to be inconvenienced by the needs or desires of others. Or perhaps my attachment is to my own worldview, which makes me unwilling to see the world through another's eyes. Perhaps my attitude of judgment and self-righteousness blinds me to the ways in which God is calling me to grow in holiness.

Whatever we love and trust comes to define us in the end, because it shapes our words and actions.

REFLECT
• What "things of the world" ensnare me?

- Am I stingy with my giving out of fear of an unknown future?
- Do I view my money as mine alone to dispose of?
- How flexible am I when things don't go my way?
- Do I try to justify my bad moods and judgmental thoughts?
- Do I recognize when God is inviting me to grow in humility and charity?
- How do I balance self-care with self-emptying?

FOCUS OUTWARD: **The Humility to Admit I Don't Know Everything**

It's human nature to get so stuck on our own idea of how things ought to be that we can't hear the perspectives of others that add depth and breadth to the discussion. We're so committed to our own vision that every issue becomes a hill worth dying upon. Some issues are trivial — think toothpaste tubes and toilet seats. Others carry more weight — the so-called liturgy wars, for instance. And then there are the really big areas of contention, the ones that cause us to unfriend others on social media.

To be poor in spirit is to be humble. No one knows everything; therefore, none of us can consider ourselves the final arbiter of right and wrong. Humility calls us to recognize the limitations of our own experience and be willing to expand our vision by listening with open hearts to the witness of others. At a more basic level, we express humility by admitting when we are wrong. It's hard to say "I'm sorry"! How often do we live with tension and unresolved conflict within our families, our workplaces, and our communities because we are unable to admit our fault or — even worse — able to admit it but unable to apologize?

It is impossible to have humility in big situations without first practicing it in small ones.

REFLECT

- Do I struggle to acknowledge when I'm wrong?
- How often do I apologize — to loved ones,

to coworkers, or in more public forums (like social media)?

- Could more frequent reception of the Sacrament of Reconciliation help me learn to admit my faults? What else could help?
- How well do I listen to others when we differ on how to solve a problem? Does my pride or vanity get in the way?

PRAY

Jesus, I've barely begun this journey of examining my heart and my conscience in light of the Beatitudes — and the first thing you ask of me is terrifying. But if humility is the gateway to holiness, Lord, help me find it. When I am bound to my own comfort; when I am imprisoned by my pride; when I allow my worldview to be shaped by these priorities rather than caring for the poor, the naked, and the stranger — forgive me.

Help me to see when I have placed my wants ahead of others' needs. Help me to say those painful words — "I am sorry," "I forgive you" — and mean them. May you be the only thing I really love, Lord — the thing that defines me, the thing to which all my other interests bow.

The Next Step

- As I read over my responses to the Beatitude "Blessed are the poor in spirit," which portions stand out?
- Which parts of my life and experience come to mind?
- Which questions speak most deeply to me?
- Is God inviting me in a new direction? What might that look like?

·· 2 ··

"Blessed are you poor, for yours is the kingdom of God." — Luke 6:20

FOCUS INWARD: **My Attitude Toward the Less Fortunate**

The modern theology known as the "prosperity Gospel" suggests that wealth is a blessing given by God to those who please him. This implies that poverty is a curse given by God to those who displease him. The trouble is, Jesus said the opposite — that poverty is the blessing. How is this so? Because those who are materially poor have no illusion that they can make it on their own. They know they need help.

It's so easy to judge the have-nots of the world: *There's a homeless camp in the woods back there? Kick them out! They're trespass-*

ing! Where are they going to go? That's not our problem! They got where they are through bad choices; let them reap what they've sown.

Stated so baldly, that attitude sounds shocking. Yet we hear these sentiments routinely, even from Christians. How reluctant we can be to undertake efforts to alleviate hunger, homelessness, and poverty. Even when we do undertake them, how often do we just drop a donation in the offertory basket, removing ourselves from the messy work?

It's as if we know, down deep, that if we get involved, we might have to admit that our own prosperity owes as much to the family, teachers, mentors, and cultural institutions that supported us along the way as it does to our own efforts. We might even have to acknowledge that such support could be all that separates our prosperity from the poverty of the guy living in a tent below the highway interchange.

Jesus challenges us to listen to the sting of conscience whispering: "As you did it to one of the least of these ... " (Mt 25:40).

REFLECT

- Do I make assumptions about people who are on welfare?
- Do I assume that most immigrants are criminals or freeloaders?
- Do I withhold assistance from the homeless because "they'll only use it for booze"? If this is a legitimate concern, what do I do instead to help them?
- Do I support (politically or financially) programs to combat poverty and homelessness?

FOCUS OUTWARD: **Getting Out of My "Bubble"**

Poverty and race are distinct issues in the modern world, but they are often closely linked. White people tend to make more money, leading to de facto segregation as they choose homes for maximum property value. Two families recently moved out of my subdivision specifically because they didn't want their kids in "that" school, the one that enrolls a high-minority, high free- and reduced-lunch population. They moved to "better" neighborhoods with "better" schools, ones enrolling more affluent — and, coincidentally, much more white — families.

We all want the best for our children: the best opportunities, the best facilities, the best support. This is a good and holy desire. But in pursuit of such goals we may isolate ourselves into a bubble. Catholics are particularly vulnerable to this because we place such high value on Catholic education. Many Catholic schools are filled with families who look and think the same. We are sometimes guilty of looking down on public schools, congratulating ourselves for our children's behavior and academic achievements. Such self-congratulation and self-isolation hamper the Church's mission. They alienate people we should invite into the fullness of the Faith.

How can we evangelize people we never meet?

REFLECT

- Do I live in a "Catholic bubble"? If so, how does this affect my ability to see those outside it through God's eyes?

- Does my lack of interaction with people poorer than myself harden my heart toward them?
- How can I protect my children from the dangers of the world without raising them to think themselves above it?
- Can my non-Catholic coworkers and acquaintances learn to know, through my words and deeds, a God who desires the best for all?

PRAY

Jesus, I know you want me to reach out to the poor around me, but it's really uncomfortable! What if I say the wrong thing? And how will I enjoy the possessions I worked so hard to obtain once I understand how little others have? I'm afraid it will change everything. I'm not ready for that.

I know not all of us are called to be Mother Teresa or Dorothy Day. Maybe it's enough to explore the fullness of the Church's social justice teachings and work to see them made reality in the world. Guide me, Lord. Help me discern your will for me, and give me the courage to act on it.

THE NEXT STEP

- As I consider my responses to the Beatitude "Blessed are you poor," which portions stand out?
- Which parts of my life and experience come to mind?
- Which questions speak most deeply to me?
- Is God inviting me in a new direction? What might that look like?

.. 3 ..

"Blessed are those who mourn, for they shall be comforted." — Matthew 5:4

FOCUS INWARD: **Grieving What Grieves the Heart of God**

The second Beatitude as presented by Matthew invites us to grieve what grieves the heart of God. Then, Jesus promises, we will be comforted. This is not a promise that our pain will be relieved in this world — earthbound suffering is real and pervasive. Perhaps comfort, in earthly terms, simply means knowing that God loves us and that heaven will be a better world than this one.

What grieves the heart of God? Every sin grieves the heart of God — all personal sins and all communal sins such as racism and discrimination. This means first of all that our own sins grieve God's heart; they should grieve our hearts as well. It is important for us to be sorry for our sins, to admit our brokenness, and to ask for God's forgiveness and healing in the Sacrament of Reconciliation.

All human suffering also grieves the heart of God. Certain grave actions — abortion, for example — spring instantly to mind. Of course, God grieves the destruction of innocent life. We aren't as quick to grieve the death of a convicted murderer, though. Or of unarmed minorities shot by police. Or the deaths of the thousands of nameless men, women, and children of every nation and race killed in wars and violence across the globe. God grieves when we harden our hearts against the suffering of his beloved children or against recognizing our complicity in communal sin.

All these things grieve the heart of God. Do they grieve our hearts?

REFLECT
- Am I sorry for my sins? Do I ask for God's forgiveness and help in resisting sin?

- Do I see beloved children of God in refugees and asylum seekers, or do I see a threat to my security?
- When victims share stories of sexual assault, do I look for reasons to discount them?
- How do I view those who protest racism, sexism, and other isms?

FOCUS OUTWARD: **Allowing Myself to Be Moved to Action by the Pain of Others**

Why is it so difficult to open ourselves up to grieving what grieves the heart of God? Perhaps it's because we recognize intuitively that once we open our hearts to the suffering of others we will not be able to deny God's call to action. We can offer that suffering up to God, but he depends on us to be his hands and feet in this world — to work for his kingdom.

For instance, once we recognize that working conditions in many parts of the world constitute grave injustice to laborers, we have to recognize how our own purchasing habits render us complicit in this injustice. We might have to change those habits in ways that are inconvenient and expensive. Recognizing that even here in the First World those working in service industries often don't earn a living wage issues a call to the business owners among us to provide all our employees just compensation and working conditions — including access to health care and time off for family illness — that respect the dignity of their labor.

Once we recognize injustice — once we allow ourselves to see the pain of others and make it our own — we are obligated to do something about it.

REFLECT
- God's heart is tender toward all his children. Is mine?
- Am I willing to embrace mourning along with God over the suffering in the world?
- Do I work for justice, even in small ways?
- Do I try to see the world through others' eyes?
- Am I called to be more generous in my almsgiving?
- Am I doing everything I can within my polit-

ical, social, and parish networks to ensure that they reflect the totality of God's vision for his creation?

PRAY

Lord, I'm realizing that an unexamined life is rife with participation in communal sins I never even considered. I'm afraid to face them, because knowledge of any injustice requires a response from me. To be honest, Lord, I'd rather hunker down in my spiritual blindness. It would be so much easier.

Help me, Lord. Help me to recognize my own sin — to admit the ways in which I am complicit in injustices that grieve you, my God. Give me the grace and the courage to be open to hear you telling me what I must change in my heart and my habits to better reflect you. Above all, give me the strength to undertake the work.

THE NEXT STEP

- As I read over my responses to the Beatitude "Blessed are those who mourn," which portions stand out?

- Which parts of my life and experience come to mind?
- Which questions speak most deeply to me?
- Is God inviting me in a new direction? What might that look like?

·· 4 ··

"Blessed are you that weep now, for you shall laugh." — Luke 6:21b

FOCUS INWARD: **Pain as an Opportunity for Growth**

No one likes pain. In fact, we work pretty hard to avoid it. We twist ourselves in knots trying to protect ourselves, and we compound the original wound by burying or denying it. We put up with issues in our marriages — or our families, or workplaces, or Church — instead of working to fix them. Why? Probably because we know it will hurt to confront the problems, and we figure it's better to tolerate a small pain than to face a bigger one head-on.

We might even think we're being Christlike — Jesus talked about turning the other cheek, after all. But suppressing our pain leads to festering resentment, which robs us of the joy God intends for us. I once had a friend who spent years trying to ignore deeply buried hurts that were blocking her from experiencing the fullness of joy in her life. When she finally began confronting those wounds, there were many tears, but also a sense that God was opening up new possibilities for her life.

It is said that cracks are the spaces where light gets in. Self-satisfied in our own strength and pride, we could walk in the darkness for years — even an entire lifetime. In fact, pain, loss, and crises *are* blessings, because they force us to face what holds us back. God wants to shine his light on our hidden wounds and heal them.

And on the far side of weeping, we often find a joy we couldn't even imagine before.

REFLECT
- What deep wounds do I try to avoid confronting? What would it take to confront them? Have I prayed for discernment?

- What weeping am I hiding from God?
- In what areas of my life do I hold God or others at arm's length out of fear of the pain of vulnerability?

FOCUS OUTWARD: **Walking with Others in Pain**

Weeping and laughter lie very close together. Anyone who has buried a loved one knows that sharing memories can provoke laughter in the midst of tears. It is healthy to express that range of emotion. Yet often, those suffering from depression, loss (of a parent, child, spouse, pregnancy), or rejection feel they must bury their pain because expressing it makes everyone else uncomfortable.

Among the best traditions of strong communities is the casserole brigade: the procession of tangible, consumable love that uplifts families during their most vulnerable times. But food may not be a person's greatest need; isolation can further deepen the pain of loss. It's natural to want to provide solutions, but nothing we say can take the pain away. Pat words risk isolating those who weep and intensifying their pain instead of easing it. Sometimes, what people most need is accompaniment, someone to be with them in their sorrow. What can we say and do to help?

- "I care about you."
- "I'm here to listen. Do you want to talk?"
- "I'm going shopping. Is there anything I can pick up for you?"
- "Can I mow your lawn for you?"

Most often, a listening ear is the greatest gift we can give those who weep.

REFLECT
- How do I respond to the grief of others?
- Do I give them the gift of my time?
- Am I willing to listen, to share their tears and laughter without trying to "fix" them?
- How can I be present to those who suffer from depression, to those who mourn a loss, to those who feel overwhelmed by illness or rejection?

Pray

Lord, so many of the Beatitudes offer a portrait of blessedness that is directly opposite human desire. I don't want to suffer. Why should I go looking for pain? Yet that is what you call us to do. You tell us, "Take up your cross and follow me."

I know that embracing my pain and the pain of others will change me for the better; it will make me more like you. But Lord, I'm afraid that all of life will be weeping, that the laughter won't come until after I die. Please give me the courage to follow you in this life, to embrace the pain and let it lead me to the laughter that follows — however long I have to wait.

The Next Step

- As I consider my responses to the Beatitude "Blessed are you that weep now," which portions stand out?
- Which parts of my life and experience come to mind?
- Which questions speak most deeply to me?
- Is God inviting me in a new direction? What might that look like?

.. 5 ..

"Blessed are the meek, for they shall inherit the earth." — Matthew 5:5

Focus Inward: **Who's in Charge?**

The word "meek" sparks an image of the geeky kid who was bullied throughout middle school. Certainly not someone we'd want to emulate! But true meekness stands nose to nose with pride and power and shows them for the bullies they are. It stands firm yet placid, in opposition to the bustle, over-commitment, and desire for control that define modern life — and it demonstrates a godlier way.

Lack of control is one of the worst things many of us can imagine. Yet to be a disciple is to live with radical trust in our God, subordinating our will to his in every facet of life, even those our culture considers off-limits — for instance, the marriage bed. We live in a culture that encourages us to impose human controls on our fertility, rather than working in harmony with the bodies God gave us.

The call to meekness challenges us to put our entire lives, even and perhaps especially the most intimate areas (like our fertility), in God's hands. It means trusting that if we, like the lilies of the field, live in harmony with his creation, he will provide for our every need.

REFLECT

- In what areas of my life do I struggle to give God space to work?
- Do I try to control every aspect of my life? In other words, do I rely on my strength instead of God's?
- How do I view the Church's teaching in favor of natural family planning and against contraception? Do I view it (or any other challenging teachings) as optional?
- Do I approach these and other issues with openness and a desire to be formed in God's will?

FOCUS OUTWARD: **We're All Cafeteria Catholics**

Cafeteria Catholicism is a malady that afflicts even those of us who consider ourselves faithful Catholics. Maybe we embrace wholeheartedly the Church's teachings on abortion, stem-cell research, and the sanctity of marriage, but when it comes to birth control, we think the Church is just out of touch with reality. Or maybe we're fully in line with every teaching of the Church on sexuality, but we close our hearts when our bishops speak out on poverty, immigration, or access to health care.

To be meek is to be willing to be guided, shaped, and formed across the board by Christ and his Church. There will always be friction between Church teachings and public policy. Perhaps we sometimes resist Church teaching because we know that accepting something means we must act on it. And action transforms us from private disciples, safely minding our own business, to evangelizers and prophets, calling out injustice and encountering all the pushback that role implies.

No matter how faithful we are, eventually we all butt against a teaching that challenges some dearly held conviction. The question is: How do we respond?

REFLECT
- When I find myself resisting a teaching of the Church, how do I react? Do I get defensive (a sure sign of the Holy Spirit pricking my conscience)? Do I blame "liberal" or "reactionary" influences, thus giving myself permission to dismiss a teaching out of hand?
- How do I handle the messiness of the intersection of faith and politics? Do I pick and choose which teachings I allow to inform my political views, so that I may comfortably align myself with one party? Am I willing to challenge my preferred party when it fails to live up to the Gospel?

PRAY
The intersection of faith and politics is messy, Jesus. I want it to be clear-cut, simple, like the

answers I put on religion tests as a child. I'd rather compartmentalize and keep my political opinions separate from my religion. Except that's not really true, is it? What I mean to say is, I want my politics to reflect my faith … at least as long as they already agree. But what about when they don't?

Give me the courage — the meekness — to dig deeply into the areas where my worldview clashes with the teachings of your Church, Lord. Guide me as I wrestle with them, and help me to find you in the midst of the mess. Remake me in your image, Lord.

THE NEXT STEP
- As I consider my responses to the Beatitude "Blessed are the meek," which portions stand out?
- Which parts of my life and experience come to mind?
- Which questions speak most deeply to me?
- Is God inviting me in a new direction? What might that look like?

·· 6 ··

"Blessed are those who hunger and thirst for righteousness, for they shall be satisfied."
— *Matthew 5:6*

FOCUS INWARD: **Turning My World Upside Down**

To "hunger and thirst for righteousness" is a powerful image. How much of our daily existence centers around satisfying our basic needs: putting food on the table; educating our children; earning the money to pay for home, utilities, and transportation? Imagine a world in which the primary motivator in every person's life was a gut-deep, all-encompassing desire to be holy. It would be a world turned upside down.

We all think we're generally good people, and we're probably right. But to hunger and thirst for God's righteousness is much more. To hunger and thirst for righteousness is to hunger and thirst for God himself. It is to spend every moment seeking God's will, even when this forces us to confront the worldly priorities — from love of comfort, to a desire for recognition, to political ideology — that have become enshrined in our hearts and determined our worldview. In other words, to hunger and thirst for righteousness is to confront and reject our idols.

If we truly hunger and thirst for righteousness, there's a good chance our world will be turned upside down. But oh, what a better world it would be!

REFLECT
- How deep is my hunger and thirst for righteousness? Is it the defining factor of my days?
- Does the all-consuming desire to be the woman or man God is calling me to be shape my every choice, action, word, and thought? Or do other desires crowd it out?
- Am I willing to change my mind and open my

heart to God's word when it stands in conflict with cherished idols?

Focus Outward: **The Church's Social Teachings**

The world can be a difficult place to navigate for those who hunger and thirst for righteousness. In these days of polarized politics, Catholics are often forced to choose between life issues and the rest of our Church's social teaching. It is a false dichotomy. The answer is not either/or, but both/and.

From Pope Saint John XXIII on, every pope has emphasized that all people, from nations down to individuals, have responsibilities to the poor and marginalized both within their borders and outside them. Church leaders have written and spoken on all the hot-button issues of the day: not only abortion and same-sex marriage, but immigration, guns, health care, environmental stewardship, unbridled capitalism, race relations, and more. The Church's social justice documents pose a great challenge to Catholics, because they demonstrate that the teachings of our Church do not align with any one political party.

No issue can be viewed in isolation. Our societal problems are like a bowl of spaghetti: tug on one strand and countless others are affected. Problems with finances, access to health care, family support, and affordable housing exert great pressure on women facing unplanned pregnancies. How can we possibly eliminate abortion without addressing these other contributing factors? In these days of polarization and acrimony, we must remember that our loyalty is to God, before country or political ideology.

The hunger and thirst for righteousness naturally turns outward. It is more than an individual attitude; it is a hunger for Godly justice for all.

REFLECT

- Do I have a pet issue that I focus on to the exclusion of all (or most) others? Who among "the least of these" are left out when I do so?

- Do I embrace the totality of the Church's social teaching? Have I formed my conscience by studying the pastoral letters, exhortations, encyclicals, and constitutions of the Church?
- Do I give my time, talent, and treasure to work for some aspect of godly justice for all?

PRAY

Jesus, the forces of hatred are strong in today's world, and I constantly find myself picking sides. It seems that we have lost the ability to listen to one another, to learn from one another. I want to be right all the time, and so does everyone else. We're so divided. That's not righteousness.

While you walked among us on earth, you demonstrated that barriers and divisions have no place in the kingdom of God. Lord, help me to remember that all of your beloved children are just as important as I am. Give me the strength to choose you and your kingdom over my idols. Awaken in me a hunger and thirst for righteousness so strong that it overcomes all my fear of wading in to work for your justice.

THE NEXT STEP

- As I consider the Beatitude "Blessed are those who hunger and thirst for righteousness," which portions stand out?
- Which parts of my life and experience come to mind?
- Which questions speak most deeply to me?
- Is God inviting me in a new direction? What might that look like?

·· 7 ··

"Blessed are you that hunger now, for you shall be satisfied." — Luke 6:21a

FOCUS INWARD: **What Do I Hunger For?**

If you are reading this booklet, you likely aren't hungry in the physical sense — in fact, quite the opposite. By some estimates, 40 percent of the food in America goes to waste. The American economy is built upon consumption — profligate, unending consumption of the next thing, the upgraded thing, the bigger thing, more things.

And yet in the midst of all this bounty, we still hunger. Our bodies and our spirits cry out for rest, or silence, or meaning, or companionship. Some people hunger for meaningful employment; others for children their bodies deny them. A famous quote from Saint Augustine captures the way we all hunger, in some way, for wholeness: *Our hearts are restless until they rest in you.*

Sometimes we downplay or deny the holy hungers within us. After all, when we have been given so much, it seems ungrateful to wish for more. But often God has placed those hungers within us for a purpose. Sometimes they reveal a divine calling. Sometimes they may simply be a cross we are asked to bear for some purpose we can't yet understand — and may never understand.

It is important to identify the hungers dwelling deep inside our hearts. Sometimes knowledge is enough to give us the direction we need.

REFLECT
- Do I listen to my deep hungers? Do I try to suppress them?
- Am I giving myself quiet, contemplative time to discern whether those hungers are a cross I must bear or an invitation to strike out in a new direction?
- In what direction do my deep hungers lead me?

Focus Outward: **Recognizing and Responding to the Hunger in Others**

Everyone is hungry for something. Consider the child who craves reassurance of his parents' love through time spent together. Consider the elderly person pining for companionship as his or her world slowly collapses due to health and mobility issues; the spouse who hungers for authentic connection; the breadwinner desperate for a tranquil space to retreat and recharge after a stressful day; the stay-at-home parent who longs for time to simply be woman or man, not caregiver. Attuned as we are to our own needs and wants, it's easy to miss the needs of others. Particularly in our own homes and families, God calls us to do what we can to satisfy the holy hungers of our loved ones.

There are hungers in the larger world, too — people hungry to be seen and heard. Women who have been assaulted or harassed, or who have suffered degradation in their workplaces and personal lives. Lonely, isolated widows and widowers. Minorities, disproportionately victims of violence at the hands of those charged with protecting them. Young adults struggling to find suitable spouses in a hookup culture. People with same-sex attractions who may have suffered a lifetime trying to suppress it and who long for affection and help in bearing the cross they've been given.

The basic hunger all share is to be seen, to be heard, to have one's experiences and suffering acknowledged. We are called to extend the compassion of Christ to all who need it.

REFLECT
- What people and situations came to mind as I read these paragraphs?
- What hungers do I see in my community? In my parish? In my home? Which ones can I do something about?
- What factors (internal or external) stand in my way?

PRAY
Lord, I don't know how to deal with my own deep hungers, let alone those of others. Some-

times I self-medicate with food, alcohol, social media, or binge-watching on Netflix — anything to avoid the crushing powerlessness of facing what I most want to hide from. But I choose to step out in faith, trusting that you have me by the hand, leading me.

What do you want this hunger to teach me? Give me the grace to embrace it — and to recognize the deep hungers of those around me. Show me how to respond with generosity when I can, and with your mercy and authentic love at all times.

THE NEXT STEP

- As I reflect on the Beatitude "Blessed are you that hunger now," which portions stand out?
- Which parts of my life and experience come to mind?
- Which questions speak most deeply to me?
- Is God inviting me in a new direction? What might that look like?

·· 8 ··

"Blessed are the merciful, for they shall obtain mercy." — Matthew 5:7

FOCUS INWARD: **Mercy Begins in the Heart**

Mercy is demonstrated through our actions, our works of mercy — like visiting the sick and imprisoned, caring for the poor and the widow. But our ability to act out mercy depends upon our hearts being open to mercy. And in modern life, mercy is not highly valued. This becomes clear every time a contentious news story appears. Whether it's racial protests, nomination hearings, or some viral video, the temptation is nearly irresistible: We make snap judgments based on our own biases and some portion of the story (but never the whole thing), and we cling mightily to those judgments, regardless of what comes to light later.

There's an adage in Catholic counseling circles: *Assume the best of the other.* If we assume the worst of others, we condition ourselves to judge those with whom we disagree instead of listening with open hearts. This prevents us from working together to bring the kingdom to fruition. When a frazzled mother yells at her screaming kid in public, we can choose to judge, or we can choose to empathize, pray, and perhaps help. And mercy does not make assumptions about people based on their weight, what they wear, what they drive, or the size of their family.

Cultivating an attitude of mercy in small matters enables us to approach larger, more difficult issues the same way.

REFLECT

- In a he said/she said situation, which am I inclined to believe?
- Who among my acquaintances — or in the larger world — do I naturally assume the worst of? To whom do I give the benefit of the

doubt? What's the difference?

• How do my biases prevent me from seeing others through God's eyes and extending mercy, as I am called to do?

FOCUS OUTWARD: **The Measure of Discipleship**

One of the most famous Gospel passages is the parable of the sheep and the goats (cf. Mt 25:31–46). The theme in the paraphrased words of Jesus is: *As you did — or didn't do — to the least of these, you did — or didn't do — to me.* This is the measure of a true disciple, and the standard by which we will all be judged on the last day.

As familiar as this passage is, reflecting on it can be quite uncomfortable. Most of us consider ourselves to be good Catholics as long as we go to Mass and confession regularly. But that's not what Jesus says matters most in the end. This isn't to say that Mass and the sacramental life aren't important. They are — vitally so! They help us grow in faith and give us strength for the work of discipleship.

However, works of mercy are what Jesus said we would be judged on. Hungry, thirsty, naked, stranger, sick, imprisoned — not one of these is pleasant to encounter. It's painful to imagine the plight of refugees and asylum seekers, of those who have suffered abuse within the Church and in larger society. Doing so puts us face to face with our own privilege, and will likely sting our conscience. Apparently, that's what Jesus wants!

Committing to the works of mercy — carving time out of schedules that are likely already overburdened — is the heart and the measure of discipleship.

REFLECT
- Where do the works of mercy fit into my life?
- Who in my immediate circle is suffering? How can I help?
- Are there ministries to the sick or imprisoned in my parish or diocese that I can support with my time or resources?
- What other situations do I keep at an emotional distance?

- Do I make room in my budget for charity?
- Do I volunteer my time?
- What social issues could I urge elected representatives to address?

PRAY

Lord Jesus, you were always clear that faith means work. These days, Pope Francis calls the Church to get her shoes dirty working in the mud. It's a powerful and very scary image. Won't I look like some privileged, cocky American with a savior complex? What if I actually am one? I'm not ready to face that.

I know, Lord. I know none of this is an excuse for shying away from people who are suffering and in need of mercy. Show me, Lord. Show me one small thing I can do to begin to serve "the least of these," and to see your face reflected in theirs. Give me the courage I need to step out and be your hands and feet in the world.

THE NEXT STEP

- As I reflect on the Beatitude "Blessed are the merciful," which portions stand out?

- Which parts of my life and experience come to mind?
- Which questions speak most deeply to me?
- Is God inviting me in a new direction? What might that look like?

·· 9 ··

"Blessed are the pure in heart, for they shall see God." — Matthew 5:8

FOCUS INWARD: **What Am I Doing to Grow Closer to God?**

We've all known people who seem to breathe holiness. Sometimes that holiness sets them on fire. Sometimes they simply exist in an aura of quiet joy. It is as if they are walking in the same world we are, but seeing an altogether different one. As if they are, indeed, seeing the face of God. How do they manage it? So often our lives feel messy, filled with conflict and negativity.

Pope Saint John Paul II's Theology of the Body boils down to this: The body and the soul are one. Whatever you do to one, you do to both; and what you do with one impacts the other as well. Put in more down-to-earth terms: What I do, I will become; what I am, I do. We will never see God in the real world until we devote time and energy to purifying ourselves, body and soul, and to looking for him. It's not enough just to show up on Sundays and holy days. We have to devote time and attention to the spiritual life, especially through praying for purity and entering the confessional regularly. We can deepen our understanding of God through participation in small groups or classes, or through solitary study.

The good news is that the moment we begin to seek God he will start revealing pieces of his plan for us. We just have to take the smallest step toward him.

REFLECT

- What does my inner life look like?
- Do I set aside time and energy for spiritual growth? Can I take a retreat weekend?
- When did I last go to confession outside of Advent or Lent?
- What kind of spiritual practice is realistic in

my life? What calls to me? Devotions, *Lectio Divina*, retreats, contemplation, spiritual direction? Reading Church documents or writings of the saints?

• What must I do in order to make this a reality?

Focus Outward: **Recognizing My Own Brokenness**

In the beginning of chapter 7 of the Gospel of Mark, the Pharisees are, as usual, baiting Jesus — this time about purity rules and defilement. As usual, Jesus sets them firmly in their place: Nothing you take in can defile you, he says. It's what's inside that counts, because what's inside comes out in the things you say and do (cf. v. 15).

Jesus presents a laundry list of sins that emerge from a defiled heart: "evil thoughts, fornication, theft, murder, adultery, coveting, wickedness, deceit, licentiousness, envy, slander, pride, foolishness" (Mk 7:21–22). And while we may exonerate ourselves from a few of these, who among us doesn't struggle with coveting, deceit, envy, pride? It can be hard to see and admit these stains on our souls. Coveting seems normal in a culture defined by consumption. Envy drives the economy. Pride looks like a virtue in a world where we idolize those who propel themselves to the top. It is important for us to consciously monitor our purchasing habits, words, priorities, actions, attitudes toward and treatment of others for alignment with the Gospel.

Only by tending to our spiritual lives can we train ourselves to see both our goodness and our brokenness with clear vision.

REFLECT

- Which of the signs of a defiled heart that Jesus lists in Mark 7 cause me to squirm?
- What in my external life signals to others that I am a disciple of Jesus Christ?
- Do I manifest covetousness through overconsumption of resources or cavalier treatment of God's creation?
- When have I perpetrated small deceptions in order to get my own way?

- When has my high opinion of myself caused conflict?
- Do my words and deeds attract others to Christ or push them away? If the latter, what must I change?

PRAY

Jesus, I keep thinking of your words: "You will know them by their fruits" (Mt 7:16). The idea that the state of my soul is visible to the world through my "fruits" is both exciting and a little terrifying. I'm just a weak, fallible human being. How can I possibly be pure in heart like you? What happens when I get it terribly wrong?

Help me learn to put you first, Lord — to set aside the time to form my heart through seeking yours. Teach me to hear your voice in the words of Scripture and your Church, and in the voices of "the least of these." Remake me in your image, Lord. Make my heart as loving and open as yours, so that I may show the world a true image of you.

THE NEXT STEP

- As I reflect on the Beatitude "Blessed are the pure in heart," which portions stand out?
- Which parts of my life and experience come to mind?
- Which questions speak most deeply to me?
- Is God inviting me in a new direction? What might that look like?

·· 10 ··

*"Blessed are the peacemakers, for they shall
be called sons of God." — Matthew 5:9*

FOCUS INWARD: **The Need for Stillness**

Isn't it interesting that this Beatitude comes so
late in the list? It's almost as if Jesus wants to
underscore that peacemaking cannot happen
until the other pieces are in place. But becom-
ing a peacemaker also depends on our ability to
hear the voice of God, the source of all peace.
And that's difficult to do, because ours is a noisy,
busy world where we fill every moment with
streaming services, social media, text messages
— the list goes on. Without silence, how can we
hear God?

As the pace quickens, we feel more and
more frantic. That morphs quickly to anger. We

become irked, annoyed, irritated, frustrated, or downright enraged — which usually gets vented to others, who react in kind. And the more conflict we enter into, the more frantic we feel; the possibility of peace recedes like a dream. The only way out of the cycle of stress and anger is to be disciplined in carving out quiet, undistracted time and space to listen for God's whisper of peace into our heart.

To become peacemakers, we must learn how to be comfortable with silence and emptiness, which gives God space in which to speak.

REFLECT
- How much of my life do I spend angry?
- Do I amplify conflict within my heart, shadowboxing my opponents?
- How long has it been since I felt God's presence in my mind and heart?
- Do I ever leave time to clear out my mind and heart for God, or do I feel compelled to fill every moment with stimuli?
- How long has it been since I unplugged altogether? Do I ever turn off my phone and simply

sit in stillness, just listening for God's voice? If I don't, how do I expect ever to find his peace in my heart?

FOCUS OUTWARD: **Pacifying Online Interactions**

There's a lot to be angry about in the world today, and everyone has a different idea of what behavior constitutes justifiable, righteous anger. In such an atmosphere, online interactions can turn toxic without warning. Who are we kidding? Sometimes they *start* that way. But being a peacemaker doesn't mean avoiding all conflict — the issues we are passionate about are contentious because they're important. Our sin is not *that* we engage; it is in *how* we engage.

In this age of memes and share buttons, it's too easy to react without thinking critically and compassionately. The information we choose to seek out, give credence to, and share online can contribute to productive conversation and the building up of the kingdom on earth. But all too often, we gravitate toward voices of outrage, judgment, and oversimplification. When we share inflammatory memes and "news stories" without fact-checking or weighing implicit biases and missing context, we contribute to a culture of anger rather than one of peace.

At the opposite end of the spectrum lies a quite different reaction to the culture of anger: a reluctance to engage or speak up at all, for fear of what people might think and what it might cost us. We cede the spiritual battlefield to the worst impulses of humanity, rather than standing up for godly holiness.

In both cases, we put worldly concerns before godly ones.

REFLECT

- Do I channel my anger over injustice in a productive way, or do I simply vent it to others?
- Do I approach online interactions thoughtfully, always keeping in mind the innate dignity of those I disagree with — and of the people touched by whatever issue we are arguing about? Am I measured, calm, and reasoned in my comments, seeking common ground

where it exists?
- Do I fact-check the memes and stories I share online?
- Do I think critically about the opinions I read, filtering them through the lens of the Gospel before I adopt them?

PRAY

Lord, there are so many potholes hiding on the road to peace. I'm angry a lot! Sometimes I just can't seem to roll with the punches. My frustration with the irritations and setbacks of life causes me to lash out at others, venting my rage at feeling impotent. But so many things aren't the way they're supposed to be. How can I help being angry?

Help me make space for your peace in my heart, so that I can bring it to all those I encounter. Help me be one who seeks solutions. Give me the grace and self-discipline to take the high road in all my interactions, honoring the dignity of everyone I interact with — even those I think are flat-out wrong. And when others take the low road, Lord, I'll need your peace then most of all.

THE NEXT STEP

- As I reflect on the Beatitude "Blessed are the peacemakers," which portions stand out?
- Which parts of my life and experience come to mind?
- Which questions speak most deeply to me?
- Is God inviting me in a new direction? What might that look like?

11

"Blessed are those who are persecuted for righteousness' sake, for theirs is the kingdom of heaven. Blessed are you when men revile you and persecute you and utter all kinds of evil against you falsely on my account."
— Matthew 5:10–11

"Blessed are you when men hate you, and when they exclude and revile you, and cast out your name as evil, on account of the Son of man!" — Luke 6:22

FOCUS INWARD: **The Cost of Being a Peacemaker**

The irony of trying to be peaceful Christians is that we are likely to find ourselves caught in conflict more often, not less. We can't stay silent in the face of the tribalism that has turned modern discourse so toxic. We must challenge the misinformation and overreactions not only of our natural opponents, but of our natural allies. To be a peacemaker is to stand between camps violently opposed to each other and take the brunt of all their rage — the justified and unjustified alike.

Perhaps this is what Jesus meant when he prepared his disciples for persecution. Insults, exclusion, denunciations — the cost of discipleship is high. It's kind of unfair, actually; surely walking more closely with God should make us smaller targets. But the opposite is often true.

On the other hand, sometimes we use too shallow a definition of "persecution." Christians often write off any challenge from nonbelievers as persecution. We find grim consolation in telling ourselves that pushback from those outside the Faith proves our faithfulness. The trouble is that sometimes — perhaps even often — such pushback comes from people who are calling us out for not living what we say we believe. Painful as it is to admit, nonbelievers are often better at spotting our hypocrisy than we are.

It can be hard to discern the difference between true persecution (a natural cost of discipleship) and justified criticism of the disconnect between what we say we believe and the things we say and do. But if we want to grow in our faith, it's a discernment we must face.

REFLECT

- What does discipleship cost me? If it hasn't cost me anything, am I really living my faith?
- On the other hand, do I allow myself to play victim? Do I view myself as persecuted, when in reality I am being challenged for a disconnect between what I claim to believe and my words and actions?
- Are there inconsistencies between my worldview and God's will for the world?

FOCUS OUTWARD: **A Christian Response to Persecution**

Persecution in the traditional sense still exists. Perhaps our first reaction to this reality should be a profound gratitude for our own religious liberty. Not merely a passive gratitude, but one that expresses itself through wholehearted participation in parish life — a recognition that our gifts and volunteering are vital to the communities we've been given. We can also stand in solidarity with those around the world who are persecuted. This may mean buying olive sculptures from the Holy Land or financing Catholic organizations that work in other parts of the world.

But at a basic level, solidarity begins with education. We may need to devote more attention to trying to understand the causes and complexities of ongoing persecution and genocide around the globe. Following Christ means opening our eyes and calling on friends and civic leaders to do the same.

This applies within our own nation, too. We should recognize domestic policies that fall short of the call of Christ, thus enabling milder persecutions. It's easy to recognize those policies in the *other* party's philosophies. It's much harder to do that with our own. Again, once we acknowledge the disconnect between a particular political position and the call of Christ, we are obligated to work for change within our party.

Of course, the minute we start challenging our friends and allies, we'll discover what it feels like to be persecuted for our faith!

REFLECT

- Do I appreciate the privilege of practicing my faith openly, without fear of reprisal? How do I show that appreciation?
- Do I give of my time and talent in my parish?
- Do I admit where my chosen political party's platform diverges from the Gospel? What am I doing to try to change that?

PRAY

Lord, the farther I go down this road, the more I realize that living the Beatitudes puts me at odds with the world. Challenging my own beliefs is hard enough; how can I possibly challenge those of my friends? Isn't there an easier way?

No, I know there isn't. You told us upfront that following you was going to cause conflict, that it would require sacrifice. This is what the cross means. Show me your way, Lord, and give me the courage to step out in faith.

THE NEXT STEP

- As I reflect on the Beatitude "Blessed are those who are persecuted," which portions stand out?
- Which parts of my life and experience come to mind?
- Which questions speak most deeply to me?
- Is God inviting me in a new direction? What might that look like?

12

"Rejoice and be glad, for your reward is great in heaven, for so men persecuted the prophets who were before you."
— *Matthew 5:12*

"Rejoice in that day, and leap for joy, for behold, your reward is great in heaven; for so their fathers did to the prophets."
— *Luke 6:23*

FOCUS INWARD: **Joy? Really?**

As we reach the end of this journey, you may be thinking, "But how can any rejoicing possibly come out of all this soul-searching and self-denial?" It's tempting, at this point, to focus on the promise of a great reward in heaven. But I'd like to share a personal story that I hope illustrates how earthly suffering can bring earthly joy.

When my husband and I were newlyweds, natural family planning was difficult. The charts didn't look the way they were supposed to: We had to abstain. A lot. Then, after we started trying to conceive, we spent years battling infertility. We pursued adoption, where we met more delays, more suffering. We raged at God. And then, for no known reason, infertility ended. It was not until the birth of our second child, who has Down syndrome, that we understood that God had used all our suffering to prepare us to welcome this child, along with all the upheaval that came with her — to rejoice in the gift that she is.

God does not manufacture trials and burdens to torment us. However, he can use the difficulties of life to teach us, to mold us in his image, to prepare us to accept and rejoice in the gifts of this world (especially when they don't fit our prepackaged vision), and also to give us a glimpse of the better world waiting for us in the life to come.

And that is worth rejoicing over!

REFLECT

- Where in my life have my crosses opened me to experiencing greater joy?
- Do I offer my sufferings to God, asking him to use them to make me more like him?
- Am I open to the joy of each moment — even the difficult moments?

FOCUS OUTWARD: **Leavening My World**

Joy is a bit of an enigma. We tend to think of it as loud and boisterous, kind of like a pep rally. But sometimes joy is a quiet emotion, a soft burn at the core of the heart, slowly but steadily melting the cold angst all around it. You could call it a stealth emotion — one that creeps outward, not demanding attention, but filtering out into the world from the one who possesses it.

If we embrace and live the Beatitudes, they change us. Bit by bit, our hearts become more like God's heart. We act more like God because we see more like God. We focus less and less on the worldly priorities that keep us chained to futility. Slowly, so slowly, those earthly chains release, and we find peace and serenity in living as we were made to live: in joy rather than in a perpetual "striving after wind" (Eccl 1:14). As we go about our days, that joy will change the world around us.

It's not that we'll never get angry or dispirited, or that we'll never weep. We will. But we will attract more of what we cling to. If we choose to dwell in anger, bitterness, and negativity, we will find more to be angry, bitter, and negative about.

If we choose the better part, seeking out joy again and again and again, it will permeate our being and overflow, attracting others to Christ.

REFLECT

- What do I dwell on and talk about in my life — the joys and blessings, or the frustrations and problems?
- How can I be clear-eyed about the brokenness in the world (and in myself) without letting it

overwhelm me?

- How does my joy, or lack of it, ripple out into my world?

PRAY

Lord, I want your joy. Remake me in your image. Help me see the world through your eyes — the things that grieve you, the suffering and weeping you ache to alleviate. Help me feel your unquenchable desire for righteousness and justice; help me understand your mercy that knows no bounds. Purify my heart, Jesus, so that I may be a vessel of your peace, able to meet opposition with grace. Teach me to cling to joy — to be so filled with it, that it flows out into the world.

Lord, I've examined my life and my world one Beatitude at a time. I can better see now both my strengths and my weaknesses. Here I am, ready to find blessedness in doing your will. Where do you want me to go?

THE NEXT STEP

- As I reflect on Jesus' exhortation to "Rejoice and be glad," which portions stand out?

- Which parts of my life and experience come to mind?
- Which questions speak most deeply to me?
- Is God inviting me in a new direction? What might that look like?

CONCLUSION

Walking Toward Blessedness

Looking back through your journal and referring back to this booklet as needed, make a list of the next steps you wrote down. These inward and outward steps of spiritual growth mark your path toward the heart of God and the blessedness of the Beatitudes. What fears or obstacles stand in your way? How can you overcome them? Is a trip to the Sacrament of Reconciliation with some new sins of the heart to confess as part of your journey?

You are on your way. Don't forget the joy!

ABOUT THE AUTHOR

Author and liturgical composer Kathleen M. Basi approaches her write-from-home career as a vocation second only to her calling as wife and mother. As a mother of three active boys and one chromosomally-gifted daughter, she moonlights as a disability advocate. She often emphasizes that writing for the Church constitutes a perpetual examination of conscience. She is the author of *Joy to the World: Advent Activities for Your Family; Bring Lent to Life;* and *This Little Light of Mine: Living the Beatitudes* (Liguori), and her music for Catholic worship is available through WLP and GIA. Her essays have appeared on NPR's *All Things Considered* and in *Chicken Soup for the Soul,* and she writes regularly for Catholic magazines.

Visit her at kathleenbasi.com.